I would like to dedicate this book to my husband, Keith, and my adult children, Hunter and Hannah. We all walked through a very similar journey when my own mother was diagnosed with early-onset Alzheimer's disease. Our family showed a great amount of support and love to her during this difficult time.

A special thank you to Maria Mughal for helping me bring this book to life with the beautiful illustrations.

My name is Hunter.
I like to play soccer.

On my next birthday,
I will be six years old
and old enough to be
on a soccer team.

My Daddy Forgets Things

A Little Boy's Journey with His Father's Diagnosis of Early-Onset Alzheimer's Disease

Written by

Celisa Bonner, LCSW

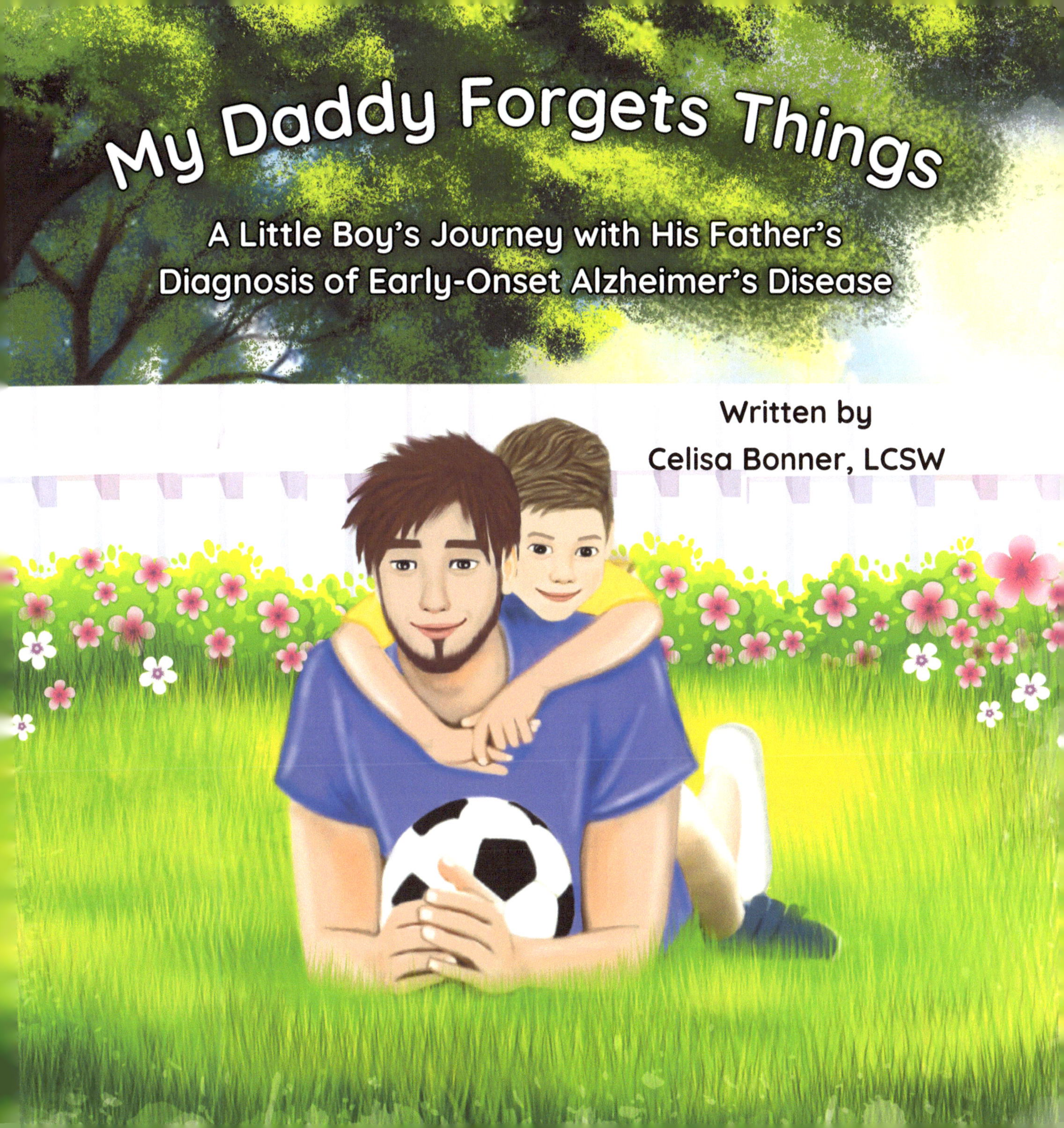

Two Penny Publishing
850 E. Lime Street #266
Tarpon Springs, Florida 34688
TwoPennyPublishing.com
Info@TwoPennyPublishing.com

Cover and illustrations by Maria Mughal.

ISBN Paperback: 979-8-8691-6755-2
eBook also available

F I R S T E D I T I O N

For more information about the author, to book her for your next event, media interview, or bulk orders, please contact: info@twopennypublishing.com

Two Penny Publishing is a partnership publisher of a variety of genres. We help first-time and seasoned authors share their stories, passion, knowledge, and experiences that help others grow and learn. Please visit our website: TwoPennyPublishing.com if you would like us to consider your manuscript or book idea for publishing.

My daddy plays soccer with me. He is the one who taught me how to play. My mommy plays soccer with me too. My sister is not old enough to play soccer, but she likes to try and chase the ball.

SCHOOL BUS
Each day I cannot wait to get
home from school because when
my daddy gets home from work,
we play soccer in the backyard.

HAPPY BIRTHDAY
Today is my birthday and I am six years old.
I am finally old enough to play on a soccer team.
My daddy is signing me up this weekend. I cannot wait!

I am on the red and white soccer team. My daddy gets
to be one of the coaches because they need extra help.
We are called Team Red. My favorite color is red.

Saturdays are when we play our games.
My papa, nana, mommy, and little
sister always come to the games.

COACH

They cheer and
clap for me. I love
to play soccer!

Today, my nana is taking me to soccer practice. My mommy is taking my daddy to the doctor. My daddy does not look sick.

My nana has been staying
with my sister and me
after school because my
mommy takes my daddy
to the doctor a lot.

My nana tries to play soccer with me,
but it is not the same. I miss my daddy.

I played my last soccer game today.
I am sad that it is over. I am also
sad because my daddy was cheering for the
blue team when they scored the winning goal.

He has never done that before. When I asked
him why he did that, he stared at me with a
puzzled look. My mommy hugged me and told
me Daddy did not mean to hurt my feelings.

When we got home,
Mommy told me why
Daddy had been
going to the doctor.

She said he was forgetting important things,
and acting different, like cheering for the other
team. He was not doing this on purpose. The doctor
said his brain was changing because it has a disease.

She said Daddy noticed these changes at first and they talked about it. He could not remember how to do important things at work that he had always done.
One time he even got lost while driving to my soccer practice.
That worried him, so he went to the doctor.

The doctor he went to knows a lot about the brain. Many tests were done to help find out what was wrong.
The doctor told him he has early-onset Alzheimer's disease. I have never heard of that before.
INTERNAL STRUCTURE OF THE BRAIN

Alzheimer's disease is not like a cold. No one can catch it. No one in our family has ever had this.

Mommy said they were surprised because they thought this was a disease that happened only when someone was older. The doctor said it could happen to adults at any age. He said scientists are studying this disease each day. My daddy was given some medicine to help him remember things. This medicine will not make him well though. He will always have this disease.

Over time, Daddy will continue to forget things like how to drive, work at his job, get dressed, and how to take medications. He may even forget my name.

Daddy will always love me even though his brain is changing. Mommy says as a family we will help him and support each other.

This makes me sad knowing my daddy is sick. I want to help him like he helped me learn to play soccer.

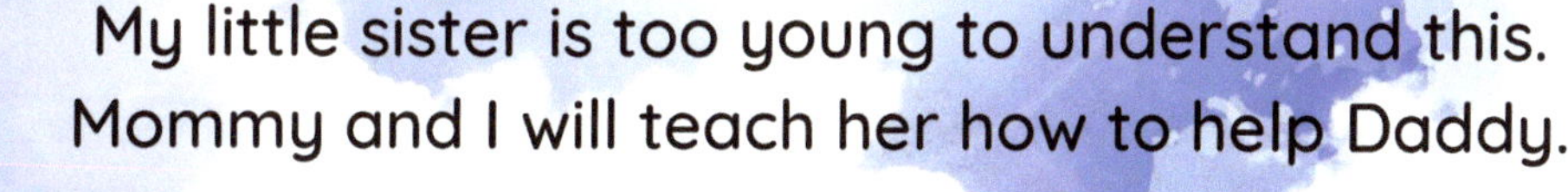

My little sister is too young to understand this.
Mommy and I will teach her how to help Daddy.

I love my daddy.

He is still my daddy,
and I am still his son.
My family will always
be there for him.

Endorsements

This excellent book provides a much-needed introduction to the changes associated with early-onset Alzheimer's disease (EOAD), written to capture the interest of elementary-school-age children. Mrs. Bonner's engaging writing style communicates practical information about this condition in an age-appropriate manner while delivering a message of hope that EOAD cannot erase the love of a parent for their child. Highly recommended!

Dr. Angela McBride, PhD

We all know someone with memory loss, but few of us know a young adult with memory loss. It is challenging for all of us to understand, but especially challenging for a child. This wonderfully written book makes it easier for a child to understand what may be happening to his or her parent and provides a tool for starting a conversation within a family.

Dr. Shannon Barsema, PhD, ABPP

My Daddy Forgets Things is a wonderful resource to help children understand the changes that may be occurring in a parent with early-onset Alzheimer's disease. Celisa uses her years of experience and knowledge in this area to present the information in a manner that a child can understand and relate to. I recommend this book to any family member who is hoping to explain an early-onset Alzheimer's disease diagnosis to young children.

Dr. Jennifer Travis Seidl, PhD, ABPP

There is a clear gap in children's literature regarding dementia, especially from the perspective of a young family member. Celisa's book fills this void. This book promises to be a crucial tool in educating young readers about dementia in an empathetic and informative narrative.

Kathleen Nishimura, Founder of Home at Last Senior Placement Services

About the Author

Celisa Bonner is a Licensed Clinical Social Worker for the Madonna Ptak Center for Alzheimer's Research and Memory Disorders Clinic at the Morton Plant Mease Hospital in Clearwater, Florida. She has personal experience with having a parent diagnosed with early-onset Alzheimer's disease. While working with hundreds of families at the Memory Disorders Clinic, she saw the need to help educate children with their parent's diagnosis of early-onset Alzheimer's disease. She authored this book to help meet this widespread need.